Especially for

_____

From

_____

Date

_____

© 2011 by Barbour Publishing, Inc.

Written and compiled by Ellyn Sanna.

ISBN 978-1-61626-319-5

Scripture quotations marked CEV are from the Contemporary English Version, Copyright © 1991, 1992, 1995 by American Bible Society. Used by permission.

Scripture quotations marked MSG are taken from *THE MESSAGE.* Copyright © by Eugene H. Peterson 1993, 1994, 1995, 1996, 2000, 2001, 2002. Used by permission of NavPress Publishing Group.

Scripture quotations marked NIV are taken from the HOLY BIBLE, NEW INTERNATIONAL VERSION®. NIV®. Copyright 1973, 1978, 1984, 2010 by Biblica, Inc.™ Used by permission. All rights reserved worldwide.

Scripture quotations marked NLT are taken from the *Holy Bible,* New Living Translation, copyright © 1996, 2004. Used by permission of Tyndale House Publishers, Incorporated, Wheaton, Illinois 60189. All rights reserved.

Scripture quotations marked KJV are taken from the King James Version of the Bible.

Scripture quotations marked NCV are taken from the New Century Version of the Bible, copyright © 2005 by Thomas Nelson, Inc. Used by permission.

Published by Barbour Publishing, Inc., P.O. Box 719, Uhrichsville, Ohio 44683, www.barbourbooks.com

Our mission is to publish and distribute inspirational products offering exceptional value and biblical encouragement to the masses.

Member of the
Evangelical Christian
Publishers Association

Printed in China.

power of faith

BARBOUR
PUBLISHING

Introduction

What is faith?

Many people think of "faith" as either a feeling or a collection of ideas that represent one's convictions. However, the Greek word most often translated "faith"—*pistis*—means "firm persuasion" and "a conviction based upon hearing."

True faith, the faith spoken of in the Bible, then goes one step further: It asks that we surrender ourselves totally to God. When that happens, our lives—how we act, how we live—will be radically, permanently changed. This is the kind of faith that has inspired so many writers and thinkers down through the centuries.

Faith is powerful. It changes the world.

And it can change you!

Faith. . .is an act of the total personality.
It happens in the center of the personal
life and includes all its elements.
PAUL TILLICH

• • • • •

Faith certainly tells us what the senses do not,
but not the contrary of what they see;
it is above, not against them.
BLAISE PASCAL

Faith is not contrary to the usual ideas,
something that turns out to be right or wrong,
like a gambler's bet: it's an act, an intention,
a project, something that makes you, in leaping
into the future, go so far, far, far ahead that you
shoot clean out of time and right into Eternity,
which is not the end of time or a whole lot
of time or unending time, but timelessness,
the old Eternal Now.

JOANNA RUSS

Faith is not belief.
Belief is passive. Faith is active.
EDITH HAMILTON

• • • • •

Without faith, nothing is possible.
With it, nothing is impossible.
MARY MCLEOD BETHUNE

• • • • •

Nothing will ever be attempted if all possible
objections must first be overcome.
SAMUEL JOHNSON

Don't waste life in doubts and fears;
spend yourself on the work before you,
well assured that the right performance of
this hour's duties will be the best preparation
for the hours or ages that follow it.

RALPH WALDO EMERSON

• • • • •

Have courage for the great sorrows of life
and patience for the small ones; and when you
have laboriously accomplished your daily task,
go to sleep in peace. God is awake.

VICTOR HUGO

Faith is a voluntary anticipation.

CLEMENT OF ALEXANDRIA

You call for faith: I show you doubt,
to prove that faith exists. The most of doubt,
the stronger faith, I say, if faith overcomes doubt.
ROBERT BROWNING

• • • • •

Far away there in the sunshine are my highest
aspirations. I may not reach them, but I can
look up and see their beauty, believe in them,
and try to follow where they lead.
LOUISA MAY ALCOTT

Faith is the substance of things hoped for,
the evidence of things not seen.
HEBREWS 11:1 KJV

• • • • •

Our doubts are traitors,
And make us lose the good we oft
might win by fearing to attempt.
WILLIAM SHAKESPEARE

Let nothing disturb thee,
Let nothing affright thee.
All things are passing,
God never changes.
Patience gains all things,
Who has God wants nothing.
God alone suffices.

St. Teresa of Avila

Faith is a bird that feels dawn breaking
and sings while it is still dark.
RABINDRANATH TAGORE

● ● ● ● ●

All I have seen teaches me to trust
the Creator for all I have not seen.
RALPH WALDO EMERSON

Build on, and make thy castles high and fair,
rising and reaching upward to the skies,
Listen to voices in the upper air,
nor lose thy simple faith in mysteries.
HENRY WADSWORTH LONGFELLOW

• • • • •

My faith demands—this is not optional—
my faith demands that I do whatever I can,
wherever I am, whenever I can,
for as long as I can, with whatever I have to
try to make a difference.
JIMMY CARTER

*But it was because the L<small>ORD</small> loved you
and kept the oath he swore to your ancestors
that he brought you out with a mighty hand
and redeemed you from the land of slavery,
from the power of Pharaoh king of Egypt.
Know therefore that the L<small>ORD</small> your God is God;
he is the faithful God, keeping his covenant
of love to a thousand generations of those
who love him and keep his commandments.*

D<small>EUTERONOMY</small> 7:8–9 NIV

A person without faith has no future.
MICHAEL J. CHEATHAM

•   •   •   •   •

The language of faith is crucial
because it affords human beings the
privilege of intimacy with the ultimate.
MICHAEL ERIC DYSON

As I reflect down the vistas of the past,
as I think about all the problems and all the
experiences I have had; without a faith in God,
a faith in prayer, and a disposition of loyalty to
God, I don't know what I would have done.

C. L. FRANKLIN

• • • • •

You can keep a faith only as you can keep
a plant, by rooting it into your life
and making it grow there.

PHILLIPS BROOKS

Faith consists, not in ignorance,
but in knowledge; and that, not only of God,
but also of the divine will.

JOHN CALVIN

• • • • •

Faith is obscure. By faith a man moves
through darkness; but he moves securely,
his hand in the hand of God. He is literally
seeing through the eyes of God.

WALTER FARRELL

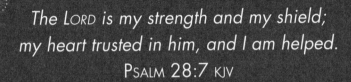

The Lord is my strength and my shield;
my heart trusted in him, and I am helped.
Psalm 28:7 KJV

· · · · · ·

Faith is an awareness of divine mutuality
and companionship, a form of communion
between God and man.
Abraham Joshua Heschel

· · · · ·

Faith is the foretaste of that knowledge
which hereafter will make us happy.
Thomas Aquinas

He that hath faith hath wisdom;
he that hath wisdom hath peace. . . .

MAHABHARATA

• • • • •

Faith means being grasped by a power
that is greater than we are, a power that shakes
us and turns us, and transforms and heals us.
Surrender to this power of faith.

PAUL TILLICH

Who created the singularity that later became
the entire universe! How did this happen!
Human beings can't comprehend it.
Human consciousness can't encompass this.

Jimmy Carter

Faith is the beginning of compassion,
of compassion for God.

ABRAHAM JOSHUA HESCHEL

• • • • •

Faith is the sense we use to perceive God.
It is also the hands we use to reveal
God to the world around us.
True faith is both receptive and active.

LEAH TOLSTOI

• • • • •

Faith is the opening of all sides and at every
level of one's life to the divine inflow.

MARTIN LUTHER KING JR.

True faith is never merely a source
of spiritual comfort. It may indeed bring peace,
but before it does it must involve us in struggle.
A "faith" that avoids this struggle is really
a temptation against true faith.

THOMAS MERTON

• • • • •

Have faith in the LORD your God and you
will be upheld; have faith in his prophets
and you will be successful.
2 CHRONICLES 20:20 NIV

Here today, gone tomorrow.
It's the best reason I can think of
to throw open the blinds and risk belief.
Right now, this minute, time to move
our faith into the grief and glory.
BARBARA KINGSOLVER

• • • • •

Believe that you may understand.
ST. AUGUSTINE

We live by faith, not by sight.
2 CORINTHIANS 5:7 NIV

I believe in the sun even when it is not shining.
I believe in love even when not feeling it.
I believe in God even when He is silent.

Unknown

•   •   •   •   •

Trusting in Him who can go with me,
and remain with you, and be everywhere
for good, let us confidently hope
that all will yet be well.

Abraham Lincoln

Faith faces everything that makes the world uncomfortable—pain, fear, loneliness, shame, death—and acts with a compassion by which these things are transformed, even exalted.

SAMUEL H. MILLER

Jesus turned and saw her. "Take heart,
daughter," he said, "your faith has healed you."
And the woman was healed at that moment.
MATTHEW 9:22 NIV

• • • • •

"If you have faith as small as a mustard seed,
you can say to this mulberry tree,
'Be uprooted and planted in the sea,'
and it will obey you."
LUKE 17:6 NIV

Faith is trust, and it is therefore
primarily volitional and emotional.
Belief, on the other hand, is primarily intellectual;
it is the assent of the mind.
But while belief is not itself faith, faith where
there is no belief is something quite impossible.

Edwin Lewis

● ● ● ● ●

Faith always contains an element of risk,
of venture; and we are impelled to make
the venture by the affinity and attraction
which we feel in ourselves.

W. R. Inge

Faith is not an easy virtue but in the broad world
of man's total voyage through time to eternity,
faith is not only a gracious companion,
but an essential guide.

THEODORE M. HESBURGH

• • • • •

Religious faith, on which sacred theology rests,
is itself a supernatural act of the human
intellect and is thus a divine gift.

MORTIMER ADLER

Religious faith is not a storm cellar to which men and women can flee for refuge from the storms of life. It is, instead, an inner spiritual strength which enables them to face those storms with hope and serenity. Religious faith has the miraculous power to lift ordinary human beings to greatness in seasons of stress.

SAM ERVIN JR.

But Jesus overheard them and said to Jairus,
"Don't be afraid. Just have faith."
MARK 5:36 NLT

And Jesus said to him,
"Go, for your faith has healed you."
Instantly the man could see,
and he followed Jesus down the road.
MARK 10:52 NLT

It is not really a question of what a man is made
to believe but of what he must believe;
what he cannot help believing.
G. K. CHESTERTON

• • • • •

Believe to the end, even if all men went astray
and you were left the only one faithful;
bring your offering even then and praise
God in your loneliness.
FYODOR DOSTOEVSKY

We have an unshakeable
commitment in an unshakeable God,
Who will never waver or tremble in
His hold on our lives.
Think of faith then as your hand
clasped in God's—
and if your grip should loosen,
know that His never will.

ARCHIBALD COURTNEY

I believe in God—this is a fine,
praise-worthy thing to say. But to acknowledge
God wherever and however He manifests Himself,
that in truth is heavenly bliss on earth.
J. W. von Goethe

• • • • •

It is simply absurd to say you believe,
or even want to believe,
if you do not anything He tells you.
George MacDonald

*And if God cares so wonderfully for wildflowers
that are here today and thrown into the fire
tomorrow, he will certainly care for you.
Why do you have so little faith?*
MATTHEW 6:30 NLT

• • • • •

*Jesus responded, "Why are you afraid?
You have so little faith!" Then he got up and
rebuked the wind and waves, and suddenly
there was a great calm.*
MATTHEW 8:26 NLT

To believe in God must mean to live
in such a manner that life could not possibly
be lived if God did not exist.

JACQUES MARITAIN

• • • • •

Belief in God is acceptance of the basic
principle that the universe makes sense,
that there is behind it an ultimate purpose.

CARL WALLACE MILLER

Faith is belief, and belief has, over and above
its intellectual character, an aspect of firmness,
persistence, and subjective certainty.
RALPH BARTON PERRY

• • • • •

My son, keep your spirit always in such
a state as to desire that there be a God,
and you will never doubt it.
JEAN JACQUES ROUSSEAU

Nor do I seek to understand that I may believe,
but I believe that I may understand.
For this, too, I believe, that unless I first believe,
I shall not understand.

St. Anselm

• • • • •

It is faith, and not reason,
which impels men to action. . . .
Intelligence is content to point out the road,
but never drives us along it.

Dr. Alexis Carrel

No one can prove God to you,
and no one can give you his faith.
Your faith may encourage mine,
and mine may inspire you, but we each
must have our own faith, one that is based not
on books or sermons, but only on God Himself.
No one but God can reveal God;
in other words, God is His own evidence.

LOIS PERNELLE

• • • • •

Faith, like a muscle,
grows stronger when it is used.

ABE BAXTER

Faith is the daring of the soul
to go farther than it can see.
WILLIAM NEWTON CLARKE

• • • • •

Faith in our associates is part of
our faith in God.
CHARLES HORTON COOLEY

• • • • •

Faith is the art of holding on to things your
reason has once accepted,
in spite of your changing moods.
C. S. LEWIS

What is faith but belief in that
which you cannot see?
St. Augustine

• • • • •

Faith is, in its essence, an act of assent—
a statement of "yes" in reply to
the question of God.
Laura Everwood

We only catch glimpses of
the world beyond this one.
Faith fills in the gaps in our vision.
ELI RUTHERFORD GRISHAM

• • • • •

Reason is our soul's left hand, Faith her right.
By this we reach divinity.
JOHN DONNE

• • • • •

Faith is believing what is beyond
the power of reason to believe.
VOLTAIRE

So often we have a kind of vague, wistful longing that the promises of Jesus should be true. The only way really to enter into them is to believe them with the clutching intensity of a drowning man.

WILLIAM BARCLAY

•   •   •   •   •

We are made right with God by placing our faith in Jesus Christ. And this is true for everyone who believes, no matter who we are.

ROMANS 3:22 NLT

Loving is half of believing.
VICTOR HUGO

• • • • •

In the midst of your doubts,
don't forget how many of the important
questions God does answer.
VERNE BECKER

• • • • •

Without risk, faith is an impossibility.
SOREN KIERKEGAARD

Faith is an act of the will,
the intellect agreeing to believe
something that lies beyond its grasp.

CHARLES DARNLEY

The only limit to our realization of tomorrow will be our doubts of today. Let us move forward with strong and active faith.

Franklin Delano Roosevelt

• • • • •

Keep your eyes open, hold tight to your convictions, give it all you've got, be resolute, and love without stopping.

1 Corinthians 16:13–14 MSG

Faith is kind of like jumping out of an airplane at ten thousand feet. If God doesn't catch you, you splatter. But how do you know whether or not He is going to catch you unless you jump out?

ANN KIEMEL

• • • • •

Living is a form of not being sure, not knowing what is next, or how. The moment you know how, you begin to die a little. The artist never entirely knows. We guess. We may be wrong, but we take leap after leap in the dark.

AGNES DE MILLE

Some people brought to him a paralyzed man on a mat. Seeing their faith, Jesus said to the paralyzed man, "Be encouraged, my child! Your sins are forgiven."
MATTHEW 9:2 NLT

• • • • •

Then he touched their eyes and said, "Because of your faith, it will happen."
MATTHEW 9:29 NLT

Faith is an assent of the mind and a consent of
the heart, consisting mainly of belief and trust.
E. T. HISCOX

• • • • •

The principle part of faith is patience.
GEORGE MACDONALD

To disbelieve is easy; to scoff is simple;
to have faith is harder.
Louis L'Amour

• • • • •

Faith is a living and unshakeable confidence,
a belief in the grace of God so assured that a
man would die a thousand deaths for its sake.
Martin Luther

One morning, I sat on cliff top high above the water,
idly watching some sea bird hover on the wind.
Suddenly, it plunged hundreds of feet,
a straight perpendicular drop to the sea far below,
where it dropped like a stone into the water.
That is faith, I thought: a total abandonment
of one's entire self, an absolute and radical
leap from one reality into another,
a headlong plunge into God.

JAMES BRANSCOMBE

And seek not ye what ye shall eat,
or what ye shall drink, neither be ye
of doubtful mind. For all these things do
the nations of the world seek after:
and your Father knoweth that ye
have need of these things.
But rather seek ye the kingdom of God;
and all these things shall be added unto you.
LUKE 12:29–31 KJV

Faith is the final triumph over incongruity,
the final assertion of the
meaningfulness of existence.
REINHOLD NIEBUHR

• • • • •

Faith is an encounter in which God
takes and keeps the initiative.
EUGENE JOLY

Faith is verification by the heart;
confession by the tongue; action by the limbs.
UNKNOWN

• • • • •

Faith is an outward and visible sign of
an inward and spiritual grace.
BOOK OF COMMON PRAYER

• • • • •

Faith is the response of our spirits
to beckonings of the eternal.
GEORGE A. BUTTRICK

Faith is a knowledge of the
benevolence of God toward us,
and a certain persuasion
of His veracity.

JOHN CALVIN

Faith is God's work within us.
THOMAS AQUINAS

• • • • •

Faith is primarily a process of identification;
the process by which the individual
ceases to be himself and becomes
part of something eternal.
ERIC HOFFER

• • • • •

Faith is courage; it is creative,
while despair
is always destructive.
DAVID S. MUZZEY

Doubt is not the opposite of faith.
Instead, we should think of doubt as
faith's natural companion, a brother in
arms who will not be dismissed until we
are at home at last in heaven.

LYLAND AELRAND

The only thing
that counts is faith expressing
itself through love.

GALATIANS 5:6 NIV

Faith is an act of self-consecration,
in which the will, the intellect,
and affections all have their place.
WILLIAM RALPH INGE

• • • • •

Faith is the force of life.
LEO TOLSTOY

• • • • •

Faith assuages, guides, restores.
ARTHUR RIMBAUD

I would rather live in a world where my life is surrounded by mystery than live in a world so small that my mind can comprehend it.

HARRY EMERSON FOSDICK

• • • • •

Accept other believers who are weak in faith, and don't argue with them about what they think is right or wrong.

ROMANS 14:1 NLT

Pity the human being who is not able to connect
faith within himself with the infinite. . . .
He who has faith has. . .an inward
reservoir of courage, hope, confidence,
calmness, and assuring trust that all will come
out well—even though to the world it may
appear to come out most badly.

B. C. FORBES

• • • • •

A person without faith is truly bankrupt.
He lacks the resources to build a life.
But even the tiniest grain of faith
can grow into something great,
taking the entire world by surprise.

LISA HOLCOMB

Faith may be relied upon to produce
sustained action and, more rarely,
sustained contemplation.

ALDOUS HUXLEY

• • • • •

Religious faith, indeed,
relates to that which is above us,
but it must arise from that which is within us.

JOSIAH ROYCE

To win true peace, a man needs to feel himself
directed, pardoned, and sustained by a supreme
power, to feel himself in the right road,
at the point where God would have him be—
in order with God and the universe.
This faith gives strength and calm.

HENRI FREDERIC AMIEL

• • • • •

It is by faith that poetry, as well as devotion,
soars above this dull earth; that imagination
breaks through its clouds, breathes a purer air,
and lives in a softer light.

HENRY GILES

A person consists of his faith.
Whatever is his faith, even so is he.
INDIAN PROVERB

• • • • •

Life without faith in something is
too narrow a space in which to live.
GEORGE LANCASTER SPALDING

If I rise on the wings of the dawn,
if I settle on the far side of the sea,
even there your hand will guide me,
your right hand will hold me fast.
If I say, "Surely the darkness will hide me
and the light become night around me,"
even the darkness will not be dark to you;
the night will shine like the day,
for darkness is as light to you.
PSALM 139:9–12 NIV

Keep your faith in beautiful things;
in the sun when it is hidden,
in the spring when it is gone.
ROY R. GIBSON

• • • • •

Faith which does not doubt is dead faith.
MIGUEL DE UNAMUNO

God to surround me, God to encompass me;
God in my words, God in my thoughts;
God in my waking, God in my resting;
God in my hoping, God in my doing;
God in my heart, God in my soul;
God in my weakness, God in my strength;
God in my life, God in my eternity;
God in my life, God in my eternity.

W. Mary Calvert

No coward soul is mine,
No trembler in the world's
storm–troubled sphere.
I see heaven's glories shine,
And faith shines equal,
arming me from fear.

EMILY BRONTË

By definition, faith is a habit, a way of life,
an ongoing commitment to say yes to God.

REGINALD GREEN

•   •   •   •   •

Faith that is based only on belief is dry and
barren. A living faith is rooted in love.

ADA GRANGER

•   •   •   •   •

Living in faith means to be informed by charity,
the love of God.

EZRA THOMPSON

What, then, is to believe in God?—
It is to love Him by believing,
to go to Him by believing,
and to be incorporated in His members.
This, then, is the faith which God demands of us;
and He finds not what He may demand except
where He has given what He may find.

St. Augustine

• • • • •

Faith is not something we give God.
It is something God gives us.

Rachel Mann

Faith is a commitment, rather than an emotion.
It is love with muscles.
JOAN MAKEPEACE

•   •   •   •   •

One in whom persuasion and belief
had ripened into faith,
and faith become a passionate intuition.
WILLIAM WORDSWORTH

Whoever is happy will make others happy, too.
He who has courage and faith
will never perish in misery!
ANNE FRANK

•   •   •   •   •

Faith of our fathers! Holy faith!
We will be true to Thee till death.
FREDERICK WILLIAM FABER

Do not seek to understand so you can believe.
Believe that you may understand.
St. Augustine

• • • • •

Faith is attitude, conviction,
and conduct based on
a right relationship with God.
It is not static, but grows in strength and depth
as we nourish that relationship with
our Creator throughout our lives.
United Church of God

You know that if you get in the water and have
nothing to hold on to, but try to behave
as you would on dry land, you will drown.
But if, on the other hand, you trust yourself
to the water and let go, you will float.
And this is exactly the situation of faith.
ALAN WATTS

Then Jesus said to the disciples,
"Have faith in God."
MARK 11:22 NLT

• • • • •

Lo! o'er ancient forms departing,
Newer rites of grace prevail;
Faith for all defects supplying,
Where the feeble senses fail.
THOMAS AQUINAS

In this faith I will live and die.
FRANÇOIS VILLON

• • • • •

We are as much as we see.
Faith is sight and knowledge.
The hands only serve the eyes.
HENRY DAVID THOREAU

• • • • •

Nothing in life is more wonderful than faith—
the one great moving force which we can neither
weigh in the balance nor test in the crucible.
SIR WILLIAM OSLER

I praise the fruit of good works,
but I see their roots in faith.
St. Augustine

• • • • •

Faith, if it hath not works, is dead.
James 2:17 KJV

Anybody who has been seriously engaged
in scientific work of any kind realizes that over
the entrance to the gates of the temple of science
are written the words: Ye must have faith.
It is a quality which the scientist
cannot dispense with.

MAX PLANCK

Give me my scallop shell of quiet,
My staff of faith to walk upon,
My scrip of joy, immortal diet,
My bottle of salvation,
My gown of glory, hope's true gage;
And thus I'll take my pilgrimage.

SIR WALTER RALEIGH

The spiritual quest is a continuous act of faith,
a faith that spiritual experience is the most
real thing in human life and that all
other categories of experience are
subordinate to the fact of God.

MARTIN ISRAEL

• • • • •

Living, active faith is confidence that
God can and will intervene in our lives.

MAUD HARRIS

Faith isn't some magical ingredient.
It does, however, lead to a confident attitude
toward God. Faith motivates our minds to the
assurance of God's power and will to act in
our lives. Faith becomes more than a mental
conviction as it grows into a commitment,
not only to trust God to involve Himself
in our lives, but to do His will.
UNITED CHURCH OF GOD

• • • • •

A living faith is not something you have to carry,
but something that carries you.
J. H. OLDHAM

Perhaps you want to know what it means to be a Christian? A Christian is a man or woman in whom can be found these three attributes which all Christians should possess: knowledge, faith, obedience; knowledge by which we know God, faith by which we believe in Him whom we know, obedience by which we render our allegiance and service to Him in whom we believe.

PELAGIUS

God has made for us two kinds of eyes:
those of flesh and those of faith.
When you come to the sacred initiation,
the eyes of the flesh see water;
the eyes of faith behold the Spirit. Those eyes
see the body being baptized; these eyes see
the old existence being buried.

JOHN CHRYSOSTOM

• • • • •

Faith aims to unite the sacred
and the profane in everyday life,
not keep them rigidly separate.

MICHAEL BARNES

Open the gates that the righteous nation may enter,
the nation that keeps faith.
ISAIAH 26:2 NIV

• • • • • •

Consequently, faith comes from hearing
the message, and the message
is heard through the word about Christ.
ROMANS 10:17 NIV

Faith always shows itself in the
whole personality.
DAVID MARTIN LLOYD-JONES

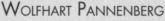

Faith as the fulfillment of life is really the
same thing as trust. And trust is one of the
fundamental aspects of human life for
every human existence. . . .
Only trust allows the soul room to breathe.
WOLFHART PANNENBERG

Faith essentially means
taking someone at their word.
DAVID WATSON

• • • • •

Faith expects from God
what is beyond all expectation.
ANDREW MURRAY

• • • • •

Faith fills a man with love for the beauty
of its truth, with faith in the truth of its beauty.
FRANÇOIS DE SALES

Faith, however, is something
that God effects in us.

MARTIN LUTHER

Faith is a gift which can be given or withdrawn;
it is something infused into us,
not produced by us.
ROBERT HUGH BENSON

• • • • •

Faith is an active, creative force.
J. H. OLDHAM

• • • • •

Faith is awe in the presence
of the divine incognito.
KARL BARTH

Faith is not a thing of the mind,
it is not an intellectual certainty or a felt
conviction of the heart,
it is a sustained decision to take God
with utter seriousness as the God of our life;
it is to live out the hours in a practical,
concrete affirmation that He is Father
and He is "in heaven."
RUTH BARROWS

Faith is nothing at all tangible.
It is simply believing God; and, like sight,
it is nothing apart from its object.
You might as well shut your eyes and
look inside to see whether you have sight,
as to look inside to discover if you have faith.
HANNAH WHITALL SMITH

• • • • •

Hope is hearing the melody of the future.
Faith is to dance it.
RUBEM ALVES

Ultimately, faith is the only key to the universe.
The final meaning of human existence
and the answers to the questions on
which all our happiness depends
cannot be found in any other way.

THOMAS MERTON

• • • • •

Faith is to believe what you do not see;
the reward for this faith is to see
what you believe.

ST. AUGUSTINE OF HIPPO

To "believe" in something is to give your heart to it. The God-life then is about giving your heart to God. Your broken heart. Your disbelieving heart. Your divided, angry, fearful heart. Your hard heart. You do not, of course, have the power to transform your own heart, but you do have the power to offer it, no matter what condition it is in, to the God who is able to make all things new.

EYLEEN FARMER

Faith keeps watch for that day,
and daily fears that for which she daily hopes.

TERTULLIAN

• • • • •

Faith makes the world what it truly is,
the creation of God.

GERHARD EBELING

• • • • •

Faith is not wishful thinking,
a pie-in-the-sky feeling that everything
will be all right. Faith is a deep conviction
that God deeply cares for us and will always
act with our best interests at heart.

UNITED CHURCH OF GOD

Faith means just that blessed unrest,
deep and strong, which so urges the believer
onward that he cannot settle at ease in
the world, and anyone who was quite
at ease would cease to be a believer.

SOREN KIERKEGAARD

• • • • •

All created things are living in the Hand of God.
The senses see only the action of the creature;
but faith sees in everything the action of God.

JEAN PIERRE DE CAUSSADE

Faith tells us of things we have never seen,
and cannot come to know by our natural senses.
JOHN OF THE CROSS

• • • • • •

It is cynicism and fear that freeze life;
it is faith that thaws it out, releases it, sets it free.
HARRY EMERSON FOSDICK

Behold, from faith thus flow forth love
and joy in the Lord, and from love a joyful,
willing, and free mind that serves one's neighbor
willingly and takes no account of gratitude or
ingratitude, of praise or blame, or gain or loss.
MARTIN LUTHER

•　•　•　•　•

I believe. . .that we ought to make a real
effort to see that the ordinary members of our
congregation understand what they believe,
and can give an answer for the faith that is in them.
GEORGE KENNEDY ALLEN BELL

As the body without
the spirit is dead,
so faith without deeds
is dead.

JAMES 2:26 NIV

It is because of faith that we exchange
the present
for the future.
NICHOLAS FERRAR

•   •   •   •   •

It is through faith that Almighty God has justified
all that have been from the beginning of time.
CLEMENT OF ROME

•   •   •   •   •

It is He alone that we seek. . .
so let us go to Him through pure faith.
ELIZABETH OF THE TRINITY

Growth in trust, in radical trust in God, is radical trust in the One in whom we live and move and have our being. Put in quite secular language, radical trust is what can free us from that self-preoccupation and anxiety that mars our lives and confines our lives. It frees us for that self-forgetfulness of faith, for that willingness to live our lives in a way that is spent in the name of a larger vision, that willingness to spend and be spent. That's what comes out of faith as trust.

MARCUS BORG

It is important to live your faith by
confessing it, and one of the best
ways to confess it is to preach it.
THOMAS MERTON

• • • • •

My faith grows stronger when I talk about it,
write about it, share it.
Like love, faith needs to be expressed to grow.
AMY BLUE

• • • • •

Preach faith until you have it.
PETER BÖHLER

We have come to the false conclusion that because faith is "irrational" (in a sense), it must then be "emotional"—and that the greater our faith, the greater will be this feeling within our breasts. This mistaken belief has led us away from the Gospel, the Good News that God loves us all. As any mother knows, true love acts even when it is exhausted, even when the only feeling in the heart is the burning desire to crawl into bed and sleep. This then is real faith: the commitment to be God's loving hands to a fretful world, no matter what we "feel."

HANNAH MAKEPEACE BROWNING

It is hard to live with broken symbols,
hard indeed to accept that the breaking
of such symbols may be a necessary
element in continuing faith.

ROBERT DAVIDSON

• • • • •

Our faith should not be in the church.
It should not be in our Christian leaders,
or even in the Bible.
When we place our faith in anything at
all besides God Himself, we create an idol.

AGNES B. FEATHERWAITE

Have faith in me when I say that the Father is one with me and that I am one with the Father. Or else have faith in me simply because of the things I do. I tell you for certain that if you have faith in me, you will do the same things that I am doing. You will do even greater things, now that I am going back to the Father. Ask me, and I will do whatever you ask. This way the Son will bring honor to the Father.

JOHN 14:11–13 CEV

There is never an act of faith without risk.
ERIC JAMES

• • • • •

Sight, or objective proof, is not the proper
ground of faith.
GEOFFREY W. H. LAMPE

• • • • •

I do not want merely to possess a faith,
I want a faith that possesses me.
CHARLES KINGSLEY

To keep your distance from the question of
[faith's] power, not to let it lay claim upon you,
not to make use of faith's power,
means to deny faith.
GERHARD EBELING

• • • • •

Real faith changes the world.
AGNES FEATHERWAITE

• • • • •

For me the greatest danger for faith
continues to be the divorce between faith
and life with its commitments.
JUAN LUIS SEGUNDO

The garment of faith we profess
must fit us also for our death.
ANGELA WEST

• • • • •

There lives more faith in honest doubt,
believe me, than in half the creeds.
ALFRED, LORD TENNYSON

Faith is not hope. Faith is the means by which we receive those things we hope for. Neither is faith sight. Faith is the evidence of things not seen. Faith can only operate in the realm of the invisible concerning those things we hope for and do not yet see. Faith cannot exist in the visible realm. When the things we hope for are manifested to our sight, then faith, the invisible "substance," having done its work, is supplanted by the visible substance, that is, the things we hope for. When the actuality comes into view, then the image (faith) vanishes.

HOBART E. FREEMAN

The life of faith is a continually renewed victory over doubt, a continually renewed grasp of meaning in the midst of meaninglessness.

Lesslie Newbigin

• • • • •

The only way to learn strong faith is to endure great trials. I have learned my faith by standing firm amid severe testings.

George Miller

The seat of faith is not in
the brain, but in the heart,
and the head is not the place
to keep the promises of God,
but the heart is the chest
to lay them up in.

RICHARD GREENHAM

Of all my prayer, may this be chief:
Till faith is fully grown,
Lord, disbelieve my unbelief,
And claim me as Your own.

FREDERICK PRATT GREEN

Never force religious instruction on your child. It is far more important for him to feel the impact of your faith. . . . If your faith is really living in you, you will not need to depend on pious words: your children will sense it in your daily life and in your contact with them.

JOHANN CHRISTOPH ARNOLD

If we use God's talents, we shall find
that they become multiplied in the use.
We thought we had two; we find we have five.
RICHARD MEUX BENSON

• • • • •

This food satisfies the hunger of the devout heart.
Faith is the seasoning, devotion,
and love of the brethren, the relish.
The teeth of the body break this food,
but only an unfaltering faith can savor it.
THOMAS AQUINAS

*By entering through faith into what God has
always wanted to do for us—set us right with him,
make us fit for him—we have it all together with
God because of our Master Jesus.
And that's not all: We throw open our doors to
God and discover at the same moment that he has
already thrown open his door to us.
We find ourselves standing where we always hoped
we might stand—out in the wide open spaces
of God's grace and glory, standing tall
and shouting our praise.*
ROMANS 5:1–2 MSG

The adventure of living has not really begun
until we begin to stand on our faith legs
and claim. . .the resources of our God.

CATHERINE MARSHALL

• • • • •

Nothing true or beautiful or good makes
complete sense in any immediate context of
history; therefore we must be saved by faith.

REINHOLD NIEBUHR

What is required of you is
faith and a sincere life,
not loftiness of intellect or
deep knowledge of the mysteries of God.
THOMAS À KEMPIS

• • • • •

The assumption that what we take
on faith we take with closed minds,
as if we had blinders on to shut out whatever
light might creep in from other sources,
lies at the root of the quarrel between
religion and science.
GEORGIA HARKNESS

*Clearly, God's promise to give
the whole earth to Abraham and
his descendants was based not on his obedience
to God's law, but on a right relationship with
God that comes by faith.*
ROMANS 4:13 NLT

• • • • •

One can believe in God with a very complete
set of arguments, yet not have any faith that
makes a difference in living.
GEORGIA HARKNESS

In David's story, we learn about strength and frailty, honor and double-dealing, humility and arrogance, all in one man. And perhaps we also learn something about our ever-surprising, redeeming and loving God, whose movement toward justice and goodness is constant, yet takes forms we never expect.

That is what the life of faith is about.

We offer ourselves to God, for the glory of God.

And we fall down, and we get up.

JOHN B. FRITSCHNER

It is better to be faithful than famous.

<small>THEODORE ROOSEVELT</small>

• • • • •

The faithful person lives constantly with God;
he is always serious and joyful:
serious because he remembers God,
joyful because he dreams of all the good
things that God has given to humankind.

<small>CLEMENT OF ALEXANDRIA</small>

If we are to be faithful to Jesus of Nazareth,
if we are to be faithful to the Gospel in the
modern world. . .in short if we are to be faithful
to our vocation as Christians, we must join
hands with people of other faiths.

WILLIAM JOHNSTON

• • • • •

Let us hang upon the lips of all the faithful,
for the Spirit of God is upon every one of them.

PAULINUS OF NOLA

Faithfulness in carrying out present
duties is the best preparation for the future.

FRANÇOIS FÉNELON

• • • • •

Help then, O Lord, our unbelief;
and may our faith abound,
to call on You when You are near,
and seek where You are found.

HENRY ALFORD

• • • • •

Our faith comes in moments;
our vice is habitual.

RALPH WALDO EMERSON

Great is Thy faithfulness, O God my Father
There is no shadow of turning with Thee:
Thou changest not,
Thy compassions they fail not.
As Thou hast been, Thou forever wilt be.

THOMAS OBADIAH CHISHOLM

• • • • •

God's faithfulness is far more necessary
than our faith in Him.

HAROLD MOOREFIELD

God the Father of our
Lord Jesus Christ
increase us in faith and truth
and gentleness, and grant us part
and lot among his saints.

POLYCARP

I hear the message, but my faith is weak:
miracle is faith's dearest child.
JOHANN WOLFGANG VON GOETHE

• • • • •

If the work of God would be comprehended
by reason, it would be no longer wonderful,
and faith would have no merit if
reason provided proof.
GREGORY I

• • • • •

The great act of faith is when a man
decides that he is not God.
OLIVER WENDELL HOLMES

Faith branches off from
the high road before reason begins.
WILLIAM JAMES

• • • • •

Faith is not rooted in the intellect,
only so far as in it requires a mental decision,
a solid commitment to proceed in a certain
direction, despite flagging emotions,
despite hardship and challenges.
Faith is not contrary to reason;
it is simply a different way altogether.
JACKSON FORD

Faith is the daring of the soul
to go farther than it can see.
UNKNOWN

•   •   •   •   •

Faith is like a blind person's white stick,
tapping ahead into the darkness where no sight
can see. We could choose to sit in a corner,
never moving because we cannot perceive
with our eyes the way ahead—
or we can learn to trust this other way of
navigating. Dare to walk into the darkness.
Take the risk!
AMY BLUE

Let us be like a bird for a moment.
Perched on a frail branch when he sings:
though he feels it bend. Yet he sings his songs.
Knowing that he has wings.

VICTOR HUGO

• • • • •

But if these beings guard you,
they do so because they have been
summoned by your prayers.

ST. AMBROSE

There are two ways to live your life.
One is as though nothing is a miracle.
The other is as though
everything is a miracle.
ALBERT EINSTEIN

• • • • •

Between us and the stars there lies but silence:
and there in the stillness let us listen to the voice
that is speaking within us.
JEROME K. JEROME

There is one thing alone that stands the brunt
of life throughout its course:
a quiet conscience.
EURIPIDES

• • • • •

*Keep your eyes open, hold tight to your
convictions, give it all you've got, be resolute,
and love without stopping.*
1 CORINTHIANS 16:13–14 MSG

On life's journey faith is nourishment,
virtuous deeds are a shelter,
wisdom is the light by day and right mindfulness
is the protection by night. If a man lives a
pure life, nothing can destroy him.

SIDDHARTHA GAUTAMA

• • • • •

There are many things that are
essential to arriving at true peace of mind,
and one of the most important is faith,
which cannot be acquired without prayer.

JOHN WOODEN

Take the first step in faith.
You don't have to see the whole staircase,
just take the first step.
MARTIN LUTHER KING JR.

Some people feel guilty about their anxieties and regard them as a defect of faith, but they are afflictions, not sins. Like all afflictions, they are, if we can so take them, our share in the passion of Christ.

C. S. LEWIS

•   •   •   •   •

Doubt is a pain too lonely to know that faith is his twin brother.

KAHLIL GIBRAN

Faith is the strength by which a shattered
world shall emerge into the light.
HELEN KELLER

• • • • •

The smallest seed of faith is better than
the largest fruit of happiness.
HENRY DAVID THOREAU

• • • • •

The faith that stands on authority is not faith.
RALPH WALDO EMERSON

All who call on God in true faith,
earnestly from the heart, will certainly be heard,
and will receive what they have
asked and desired.

MARTIN LUTHER

• • • • •

Faith crosses every border
and touches every heart in every nation.

GEORGE W. BUSH

• • • • •

A better world shall emerge based
on faith and understanding.

DOUGLAS MACARTHUR

Faith is the highest passion in a human being.
Many in every generation may not come
that far, but none comes further.

SOREN KIERKEGAARD

• • • • •

Is it faith to understand nothing,
and merely submit your convictions
implicitly to the Church?

JOHN CALVIN

We speak the language of miracles
by remembering our faith in the unseen
world of God. The intangible works of God
become tangible through the power
of our faith to step forward when we feel a
gentle nudge to be a friend to someone in need.
When we act upon the creative power of God
dwelling within us, we demonstrate faith in
action and the miracle of human life.

VICKY THOMPSON

It's faith in something and enthusiasm for
something that makes a life worth living.
OLIVER WENDELL HOLMES

● ● ● ● ●

Faith means belief in something concerning
which doubt is theoretically possible.
WILLIAM JAMES

And the attitude of faith is the very opposite
of clinging to belief, of holding on.
ALAN WATTS

• • • • •

Faith is much better than belief.
Belief is when someone else does the thinking.
RICHARD BUCKMINSTER FULLER

• • • • •

Doubt is not the opposite of faith;
it is one element of faith.
PAUL TILLICH

I may have the gift of prophecy.
I may understand all the secret things
of God and have all knowledge,
and I may have faith so great I can move
mountains. But even with all these things,
if I do not have love, then I am nothing.
1 CORINTHIANS 13:2 NCV

• • • • •

I have not lost faith in God.
I have moments of anger and protest.
Sometimes I've been closer
to Him for that reason.
ELIE WIESEL

If you desire faith,
then you have faith enough.

ELIZABETH BARRETT BROWNING

If fear is cultivated, it will become stronger.
If faith is cultivated, it will achieve mastery.
JOHN PAUL JONES

• • • • •

Faith is what someone knows to be true,
whether they believe it or not.
FLANNERY O'CONNOR

Choose your friends with caution;
plan your future with purpose,
and frame your life with faith.
THOMAS S. MONSON

•   •   •   •   •

The mysteries of faith are degraded if they are
made into an object of affirmation and negation,
when in reality they should be
an object of contemplation.
SIMONE WEIL

If we were logical, the future would be bleak,
indeed. But we are more than logical.
We are human beings, and we have faith,
and we have hope, and we can work.

JACQUES YVES COUSTEAU

● ● ● ● ●

Amidst the confusion of the times,
the conflicts of conscience,
and the turmoil of daily living,
an abiding faith becomes an anchor to our lives.

THOMAS S. MONSON

And I will raise me up a faithful priest, that shall do according to that which is in mine heart and in my mind: and I will build him a sure house; and he shall walk before mine anointed for ever.

1 SAMUEL 2:35 KJV

Faith in God's revelation has nothing to do with an ideology which glorifies the status quo.

KARL BARTH

• • • • •

May it not be that, just as we have to have faith in Him, God has to have faith in us and, considering the history of the human race so far, may it not be that "faith" is even more difficult for Him than it is for us?

W. H. AUDEN

The only faith that wears well and
holds its color in all weathers is that which
is woven of conviction and set with the
sharp mordant of experience.

JAMES RUSSELL LOWELL

● ● ● ● ●

Blind faith, no matter how passionately expressed,
will not suffice. Science for its part
will test relentlessly every assumption
about the human condition.

E. O. WILSON

What if some were unfaithful?
Will their unfaithfulness nullify God's
faithfulness? Not at all! Let God be true,
and every human being a liar.
ROMANS 3:3–4 NIV

• • • • •

My reason nourishes my faith
and my faith my reason.
NORMAN COUSINS

From faith, hope, and love,
the virtues of religion referring to God,
there arises a double act which bears
on the spiritual communion exercised
between God and us; the hearing
of the word and prayer.

WILLIAM AMES

If you find a thing difficult, consider whether it would be possible for any person to do it. Because anything that is humanly possible, that falls within human capabilities— you, too, can accomplish.

MARCUS AURELIUS

• • • • •

There is only one God, and he makes people right with himself only by faith, whether they are Jews or Gentiles.

ROMANS 3:30 NLT

If we fight with faith we are twice armed.
PLATO

• • • • •

Be faithful in small things:
it is in them that your strength lies.
MOTHER TERESA

• • • • •

Whoever reflects earnestly on the
meaning of life is on the verge
of an act of faith.
PAUL TILLICH

*Without question, this is the great
mystery of our faith: Christ was revealed in
a human body and vindicated by the Spirit.
He was seen by angels and announced to the
nations. He was believed in throughout the
world and taken to heaven in glory.*
1 Timothy 3:16 NLV

• • • • •

Pray inwardly, even if you do not enjoy it.
It does good, though you feel nothing.
Yes, even though you think
you are doing nothing.
Julian of Norwich

If you have built castles in the air,
your work need not be lost; that is where they
should be. Now put the foundations under them.
HENRY DAVID THOREAU

• • • • •

We do not believe in immortality
because we can prove it, but we try to
prove it because we cannot help believing it.
HARRIET MARTINEAU

Faith is there when a person turns
and smiles at you when you're feeling down.
Faith touches your heart when a child
reaches up to give you a hug. Faith says,
"Look over here!" when you are lost and can't
find your way. Faith is the power of God
guiding you home to His ever-presence.

VICKY THOMPSON

Faith is an excitement and an enthusiasm:
it is a condition of intellectual magnificence
to which we must cling to as to a treasure,
and not squander on our way through
life in the small coin of empty words,
or in exact and priggish argument.
GEORGE SAND

• • • • •

Faith is the refusal to settle for anything
but everything: the utter fullness of God.
LISA TRUEBLOOD

Then he said to Thomas, "Put your finger here;
see my hands. Reach out your hand and put
it into my side. Stop doubting and believe."
Thomas said to him, "My Lord and my God!"
Then Jesus told him, "Because you have seen
me, you have believed; Blessed are those who
have not seen and yet have believed."

JOHN 20:27–29 NIV

The relationship between the believer and God is framed in terms of an ancient client-patron relationship. As God's "clients" to whom He has shown unmerited favor (grace), our response should be. . .a "constant awareness" of prescribed duties toward those in whom we are indebted (God) and the group in which we are embedded (God's kin group, the body of Christ). This "constant awareness" is the expression of our faithfulness. . . . "Faith" is not a feeling, but our pledge to trust, and be reliable servants to, our patron (God), who has provided us with tangible gifts (Christ) and proof thereby of His own reliability.

J. P. HOLDING

For me, theology is the consciousness
that a community or a Christian generation
has about its faith at a given moment.
Theologies are called upon to succeed one
another: they are successive
understandings of faith.

GUSTAVO GUTIÉRREZ

• • • • •

Fear imprisons, faith liberates;
fear paralyzes, faith empowers;
fear disheartens, faith encourages;
fear sickens, faith heals;
fear makes useless, faith makes serviceable.

HARRY EMERSON FOSDICK

The only limit to our realization of tomorrow
will be our doubts of today.
Let us move forward with strong and active faith.
Franklin Delano Roosevelt

• • • • •

It is only when God speaks and awakens
human faith that the natural object becomes
sacramental. But this can happen to material
things only because this is a sacramental
universe, because God created all
things visible and invisible.
Donald M. Baillie

There is one inevitable criterion of judgment touching religious faith. . . . Can you reduce it to practice? If not, have none of it.

HOSEA BALLOU